FROM **BROKEN** TO *Beautiful*

❖

A Memoir in Poetry

CYNTHIA R. HARRIS

authorHOUSE®

AuthorHouse™
1663 Liberty Drive
Bloomington, IN 47403
www.authorhouse.com
Phone: 1 (800) 839-8640

Published by AuthorHouse 12/27/2019

ISBN: 978-1-7283-3505-6 (sc)
ISBN: 978-1-7283-3504-9 (e)

DEDICATION

My dedication page may seem unusual, but I'm dedicating it to my Heavenly Father. I thank God that He has blessed me with the gift, this talent, of writing. It wasn't until about a year ago that I started to believe in myself, and believe that I could actually write a book and publish it. I thank God for His wonderful plans for me and I thank Him for not giving up on me.

I can definitely say He has influenced me to write the poems written in this book. Even in the dark-themed poems, He still was with me, giving me the strength to write. Not only has God influenced me to write this book, but He has also done some healing within me while I was in the process of writing this book.

Because I know this is God's plan for me, I know I will meet success! God is such a wonderful, faithful, and patient Father, and I know He's with me.

Thank you God for walking with me as I walk with you.

CONTENTS

FOREWORD

I never thought I would be writing a book and getting it published. Here I am, 32 years of age, and my dreams are coming true. Who would have thought, I'd be sharing my poetry with the world!?

I have been writing poetry for as long as I can remember. I started young; I don't think I was a teenager when I started writing. I'm surprised, yet so very thankful, that I am still writing. This is a talent/ gift that God has put in me, and He's seeing to it that I share it with the world.

The purpose of this book is to encourage those struggling with their relationship with God. It's for those who enjoy reading poetry. My book is for giving an awesome view of God that some may not have thought of Him before, using poetry. I broke it up into two sections. The first part is about me and my struggles, the darkness I was in, and my search to find God. In the second part, it shows how God has always loved me, the healing I've experienced and the happiness I have now found.

The first part of my book is poetry I wrote when my life was going downhill. I was in disobedience, in sin, and God felt so distant. I took my pain, the darkness, and wrote about it. The latter part of my book is when my life was in delight and in awe of God. He encouraged me, and picked me up when I repented. When I finally made up my mind, and made the decision to follow and trust Him, things got a lot brighter. I wrote about His amazing, forgiving, and loving ways.

Furthermore, there are a few pieces that will inspire the unbeliever, or the backslider. There is encouragement for those who are seeking to marry. I've written something about that too. There are no limits!

My book is for an audience of every race/ethnicity, anyone from any socioeconomic background, all students of every level of education, and every person working in any profession. This book will encourage all!

ACKNOWLEDGEMENTS

I would like to acknowledge and thank Author House for their help and support. The team that assisted me in this process has been absolutely amazing! Thank you all so very much!

I would like to thank my family and friends, who have lovingly supported me, genuinely, truly believed in me, and believed I could do this. Hey, thank you all so much for pinching in to help me accomplish this great goal of mine! May God truly bless you all abundantly!

I would also like to thank every person that said:

"I love your writing!" and "I love your poetry!" YOU have inspired me to continue to keep writing.

And to anyone else I may have left out, Thank you all so very much!

BEFORE THE CYN (SIN)

CRYING OUT TO GOD

God, I feel like I'm trapped inside of a box with no way out. I turn to the right, to the left, try to go forward and backward, but I can never break out.

I'm so stuck in my mind and ways; I need You to change my heart
I'm trapped inside of this mess and I need You to give me a brand new start.

Father God, I'm so sorry that I'm failing You and that my heart is so weak
I'm sorry I'm not growing and that all of what I see for me is bleak...

I'm ashamed now of how I turned out; I never thought my life would be like this
I always thought I'd be the person You wanted, living in holy spiritual bliss.

I'm so tired of crying myself to sleep at night
I just want to be happy; I just want to be alright.

None of this even seems real to me; it feels so surreal
I'm out of touch with heaven's reality; I'm not even sure anymore of how I feel.

I'm so numb; I don't even recognize why I hurt anymore
I'm so numb; I don't even recognize what I'm in anymore.

Please God, please save me and rescue me
Please make haste to help me, so I can feel and see Your glory.

20 years of chaos and pain - 20 years of tears and no gain
Time is up, but before You come, please give me joy again
Time is running out, but before eternity is here, please return hope unto me again.

A POEM LETTER TO GOD

Dear God, I feel that my cries and voice go unheard

I know You can hear me, but I feel like all my trying is being put out to the curb

Father, I don't know what else I can do to get out of this

So please make haste to help me, because Your will for me I don't want to miss.

Please Father God I'm so tired of being lost and confused...

God, I'm tired of the dark painful days and all of the abuse

I act out to get help and attention, but everyone overlooks it

I cry out to You, but it seems though, to no benefit

So please God help me, I have nowhere else to turn

Please get me out of this, heal and save me because I don't want to burn.

What do You want me to do? I'm desperate for anything.

Eager to be changed, I'll do what You will, if it's freedom, healing, and Your joy it'll bring.

Please don't cast me out, count me down, or be upset with me.

God please, I just need Your help, to save and strengthen me for victory

I'm so frustrated, I have so much to say, yet no words at all because I'm in spiritual decay.

So Father God, I'm calling out to You again; please answer my cry.

Help me and save my soul, free me and fill my life before I die.

GOD IS BIG ENOUGH ...
HE CAN TAKE IT!

Do You hurt when I hurt
Do You cry when I cry
Do You feel what I feel?

I'm sorry I put You through hurt
I'm sorry I made You cry
I'm sorry for the pain You felt.

You said You'd wipe away every tear and put them in a jar
You said You'd always be with me, always near and never far.

I don't feel Your presence and I can't hear Your voice
But You still love me regardless, by choice.

I feel like I failed You and I feel as if I let You down
I just pray and hope my sorrow days will turn around.

Please don't be mad or upset at me, and don't take away Your Holy Spirit
from me, nor the blessings You have for me, away;
Please just continue to wait for me until I'm completely changed at that
designated day.

I'm sorry my love for You isn't good, that I couldn't love You enough to
count on You
I'm sorry I never fought hard or good enough to prove that I do have a
love for You.

I'm sorry I fall short everyday and I'm not good at pleasing You
I'm sorry I wouldn't accept Your love; I'm sorry I blocked You.

Always thinking of the bad and how I thought You weren't ever there for me;
I'm sorry I put You in the "this person has hurt me too" category.

I'm sorry and I feel bad for the way I treated You, and behaved
I'm sorry for mistreating You and denying the love to me You gave.

I'm sorry I struggled to realize that You are a good God
I'm sorry I turned my back on You, thinking You weren't a good God.

I'm sorry I've hurt You so bad; please accept my apology
I'm sorry for all the wrong things I've thought about You; please accept
my apology.

I want to show You that I do love You
I want to feel love so I can give it to You

Teach me and show me what You like and how to love You
Teach me and show me what I can do to prove the love I have for You.

I'm so damaged, I'm full with hurt and pain
My heart is in sorrow, it's just peace and joy that I want to gain.

So please God accept this offer and my plea
Please accept and like this poem as my apology.

Please forgive me Father, I'm Sorry. I do love You.
Forgive; I'm sorry; I want to truly love You.

AFTER THE CYN (SIN)

YOU ARE THE ONLY ONE.
THERE IS NO ONE LIKE YOU

You are the only one that will always answer my call.

You are the only one I can fully, wholly trust; I know no other like You.

You are the only one that will never let me down.

You are the only one that truly cares about me.

You are the only one that truly cares for me.

I know no other like You.

You are the only one that will never forget me.

You are the only one who thinks the most highly of me and invests the most confidence in me.

You are the only one that that will always release to me the things that I need.

I know no other like You.

You are the only one who will always help me and not hurt me.

I know no one like You.

I will thank You and worship You with tears streaming down my face, with oil anointed on my head, and with the blood that was shed from Your hands and feet.

There is no one like You!

SERENITY

You wiped my tears away every time I cried

When I was in darkness Your light, to me, You supplied.

You picked me up every time I fell down

Taking my fallen position and turning it around.

Having doubt, unbelief, and fear; You caused me to trust You

Giving me help, peace, and comfort; You gave me a reason to continue.

When I cried out to You at night in my bed; You came down to hold me

Providing compassion and sweet, sound, heavenly sleep; You held me until the morning

Washing away every unfruitful and evil being inside my heart; cleaning me up

Downloading what's good and pure into my heart, leaving no room for darkness to interrupt.

Thank You for all You have done for me, and thank You for what's to come

I know where my help, strength, and joy comes from!

WHAT HE HAS DONE FOR ME

For You have loved me with an everlasting love
For You have drawn me with Your loving kindness
You have cleansed me with Your grace and mercy
For You have clothed me with your righteousness.

Blood was shed to save me from Your wrath
Holes were drilled to save me from death
Being hung high so I wouldn't have to be without
Underneath for three days so my sins could be buried and blotted out.

Raised to new life so I can live
Seated in majesty watching over me
Reconciled me to the Father so I can commune with Him
Praying on my behalf, interceding for me.

For You have loved me with an everlasting love
Your thoughts and heart are consumed with loving me
For You have drawn me with Your loving kindness
It is Your very nature to take care of me.

You have cleansed me with Your grace and Your mercy
Leading and guiding me so I will never be alone
For You have clothed me with Your righteousness.

You are my Lord. You are my God. You are my King.
You care, love and bless me.

ALL BECAUSE

When I am afraid, You hold me
When I am lost, You guide me
When I am lonely, You comfort me and
When I am angry, You soothe me.
All of this because You love me.

When my heart is hurting, You mend it
When my mind is racing, You sound it
When my spirit is low, You lift it and
When my soul is wounded You heal it.
All of this because You love me.

When things are getting too hard for me, I praise You
When the circumstances are becoming too tough, I sing to You
When I don't know where to go or what to do, I pray to You and
When I'm confused and hopeless, I worship You.
All of this because I love You.

When my feelings are hurt, I meditate on You
When my life seems purposeless, I seek You
When my world is out of whack and stagnant, I come to You and
When my reality is dark and grim, I read about You.
All of this because I love You.

Rain or shine, You open the heavens above me
Snow or clouds, Your Spirit still shines in and through me
Smile or frown, Your love encompasses me
Wrong or right, Your mercy keeps me
Right or left, Your grace guides me

And all of this...

Because of L. O. V. E...

Because You love me!

A LOVE SONG TO THE LORD

I love You Lord, for You have set me free

I love You Lord, for You give me victory.

I love You Lord, for You always love me

I love You Lord, for You give me all good things unconditionally

I love You Lord, for You have healed my heart

I love You Lord, for You are always with me; we'll never be apart.

I love You Lord, for You have renewed my mind

I love You Lord, for I am Yours and You are mine.

I love You Lord, for You have filled my heart

I love You Lord, for You loved me from before the start

I Love You Lord, for You; yes, You are my rock!

I love You Lord, for Your love, mercy, and grace, for me never stops

I Love You Lord, for You make the sun shine on me from above

I love You Lord, for You rain down, on me Your heart of love.

I love You Lord, for You have restored my soul

I love You Lord, for I will serve You until I am gray and old.

I love You Lord, for You give me joy and peace

I love You Lord, for only with You do I wish to spend eternity.

GROWING UP FOR SPIRITUAL MATURITY

I'm ready and prepared to give Him all of my life

I'm ready and prepared to give Him all of my trust

I'm ready and prepared to give Him all of who I am

I'm ready and prepared to do all that I have to do for me to be closer to Him

I'm ready and prepared to do all that is necessary for me to feel Him close to me.

I'm ready and prepared to...

..Do all and whatever it takes for God to be proud of me:

Letting go fears

Letting go uncertainty

Letting go of the things that I think I need so badly

Letting go of the people who I care for, but don't do me any good

Letting go of sexual desires that I think I need

Letting go of everything that I have held onto knowing that they haven't propelled me forward

I have to be the person God needs me to be, by letting go, and being ready and prepared.

PUT ME FIRST

Put Me first. For what can man do for you?
Put Me first. I know all you need
Put Me first. For what yourself, can you do?
Put Me first. I teach you how to succeed.

Put Me first. For I know the desires of your heart
Put Me first. I already know the things you want to ask
Put Me first. For I loved you from before the start
Put Me first. I provide the provision so what you'll have will last.

Put Me first. Seek after Me.
Put Me first. Trust in Me
Put Me first. Have faith and hope in Me
Put Me first. For there is nothing too hard for Me!

Put Me first. I clean the heart
Put Me first. Nothing can pull My love for you apart
Put Me first. I need you to heal
Put Me first. Believe that I am real!

Put Me first. There's a work for you to do
Put Me first. Keep coming to Me because I'm not through.
In all your doing, Keep Me First.
And watch your dreams come true.

Watch the healing in your heart that I will do
Watch the favor over your life like never before
Watch as I open those once shut doors.

Put Me first. Keep Me first.

"NO MORE HIDING" (COME OUT)

I see you hiding behind the hurts and pains of your heart
Didn't you know that I knew all about that even before the start?
You're hiding because of what was done to you
Come out from there and receive the healing I have for you.

You're like a little child, so innocent, hiding behind a tree
There's no more need to hide My child, I have all of what you need
There are levels of depths of the sorrows that you carry
You hide to protect yourself from harm, but don't you know My liberty
for you, I will not tarry.

Come out of your hiding place and feel My love
Stop hiding behind that tree and experience the freedom that comes
from above
I need you to stop hiding so I can come in
Come out of that place so every hurt I can mend.

Don't you know that I will never hurt you?
I will never harm you My child; I love you for infinity times two.
So no more hiding, come out;
Seek Me and you will find what My love for you is all about!

FAITHFUL REWARDER

I see you diligently seeking beyond what you can see
You're searching for Me further than what your mind can perceive.
Know that I watch your every move; nothing escapes My eye
Those things you long to know, I will provide.

Reading day and night, and night and day
This world's busiest pace doesn't keep you away
Praying and more praying to get closer to Me
In due time you will birth that deep intimacy that you long seek from Me.

Blessings will begin to fall as you walk in obedience to My word
Continue to dive deeper into Me and I'll reveal the secrets in this earth
that have occurred.
The windows of Heaven will begin to open as you live in My ways
Through this, the world will see just how much a Christian life is worth
living; it pays!

Countless of numerous benefits you will attain
Just by staying before Me; upon your life will this advantage always
reign.
I've seen you cry out to Me repeatedly for you to be clean
Your desire to be free is what My grace is for, so you can be dirt free
indeed.

Just be still and continue to do what you're doing; for I shall reward.
For your eyes have not seen, your ears have not heard, nor has it entered
into your heart, My child, what I have in store!

NEVER LEAVE. NEVER FORSAKE

Haven't I told you that I will never leave you and that I will never
forsake you?
In the darkest of valleys,
On the loneliest of mountains,
In the deepest deserts,
In the middle of lost,
In the scariest of moments,
When surrounded in depression and despair,
While covered in filth and dirty rags,
When the bills are due,
When you're homeless,
When the car stops working,
When your loved one passes,
When your heart gets broken:

I said I will never leave you nor will I ever forsake you!

FOR BACKSLIDERS
AND UNBELIEVERS

NAMES OF GOD

Jehovah Elohim - Strong Creator
You love and give freely; You are not a dictator.

Jehovah Elyon - Lord Most High
You are the only one; there is a true living, real God, in the sky.

Jehovah Adonai - Lord, my Master
You give us all answers and *guide* us; Your Word is our forecaster.

Jehovah Rapha - Lord, my Healer
You are ever present. You do exist; there's no other God that's real.

Jehovah El Olam - Everlasting God
You're my protector; You comfort me with Your staff and rod.

Jehovah El Roi - God Who Sees
For You know all about me, You know everything, and meet all of my needs.

Jehovah Sabaoth - Lord of Host
You're the One that I chase and run to, and after, the most.

Jehovah Richi - Lord my Shepherd
You look over me - so closely like a mother leopard.

Jehovah Tsidkenu - Lord my Righteousness
You're the One that cleanses me to present me Holy on Your day, so that at Your coming, I won't miss.

Jehovah Shalom - Lord my Peace
Your grace is sufficient; You calm all the storms in my life and cause them to cease.

Jehovah Chereb - Lord our Sword
You send Your army of angels to protect and keep over me; they move immediately, working on my behalf all in one accord.

Jehovah El Kanna - God that is Jealous
I'm hungry for You and search after You; for You I am zealous.

Jehovah Ezer - Lord my Help
You do all that I cannot; You do it all for me because I can't do it myself.

Jehovah Avinu - Lord, my Father
There is no one on this Earth that can do for me as You can. -No I don't even bother to ask!

Jehovah Hashopet - Lord, my Judge
You balance my life.

Jehovah Ori - Lord, my Light
Your love shines on and through me; putting every dark thing in me, out of sight.

Jehovah El Gibbor - Mighty God
You are the same yesterday, today, and forever. Your might is everlasting; it's not a façade.

Jehovah Immeka - The Lord is with you
He promised to never leave, to never forsake; He didn't choose you by mistake.

Jehovah Selichot - God of Forgiveness
You continued to love me, even while dressed in filthy rags and while in a sinful mess. And you clothed me in a pure white dress.

Jehovah Jireh - Lord, my Provider
You promised to send The Comforter who will always be with me; You promised to walk with me, side-by-side.

WHO WERE YOU? WHO ARE YOU?

He was with Noah: sparing him and his family
He was with Abraham: blessed him beyond measure
He was with Jacob: he fought to receive a blessing
He was with Joseph: his brothers couldn't kill him
He was with Moses & the Israelites: the Red Sea couldn't overtake them
He was with Joshua: he grew in strength and courage
He was with Ruth: the Davidic line was conceived
He was with David: his bloodline will birth the Savior
He was with Solomon: the wisest man in his time
He was with Nehemiah: rebuilding the walls of Jerusalem
He was with Esther: to save His people
He was with Job: he increased double
He was with Isaiah: prophesied of the coming king
He was with Jeremiah: the potter and the clay
He was with Ezekiel: dry bones will live again
He was with Daniel: the lions couldn't eat him in the den
He was with Shadrach, Meshach, and Abed-nego: the fire couldn't consume them
He was with Joel: God will restore the years, and pour out His Spirit upon all flesh
He was with Amos (and all the other prophets): mouthpiece for God's coming judgment
He was with Jonah: the fish couldn't eat him
He was with John: be ye baptized
He was with Paul: radicalism for Christ!
He was with Stephen: dying for Christ, afterwards returning to glory
He was with Jesus: death couldn't take Him!

Who were you? Who are you?

Can God not change you?

Can God not take the bad in your life and turn it for your good?

Is there anything too hard for God?

So who were you before God got a hold of you? And so, who are you now?

THE ONLY ONE

To the Unbeliever
You cringe at the sight and the sound of His name. You repudiate the being of the only Truth. You'd rather effectuate your own self-fulfilling prophecies rather than concede to the only One that is The Way, The Truth, and, how I like to say it, The Life and Light. And you chose to succumb to the ways of the world. Why? Why disembody yourself from The One that's here to love you unconditionally, take care of you, and help you, unconditionally? To guide you. To instruct you. To teach you. And to lead you. When will you stop being deceived and come into the Truth already!? Stop looking at MAN and then blaming God. But rather look at God and help man.

WILL YOU BELIEVE IN
MY SALVATION?

My blood ran red for you on the cross
My wrists and ankles became pierced for you
I was hung up high nearly naked with just a wrap going across
By doing this I showed you no one else can love you as much as I do.

The world wants you to think that I'm the bad guy, and not to believe in Me
But I was beaten beyond recognition to set you free
Man says that I'm a myth and that I don't exist
But who creates and gives life? You will find that it's My Spirit in the midst!

My body was severely bruised to bring you in
My head was crowned with thorns
I took what no other could bare to endure, to erase and destroy your sin
To not go through with this, keeping you bound, this I could not condone.

Being walked up to the top of the mountain, carrying the cross on My back
Do you understand to not have sin rule over you, take My yoke upon you and do not slack.

Raised to new life so you can live it abundantly
To decline My truth is Hell, so please believe in Me.

MARRIAGE

DEAR FUTURE HUSBAND

I'm trusting God for you.
He told me that you will come and I believe that's true.

For He will lead you to me.
And once you're here, you will lead me into His glory.

I have no need to search and look.
All I'm searching for is the Lord, and I'll know how to be with you by reading it in His book!

I will not be alone and lonely as I wait.
I'm learning my purpose and you are too, so once together we'll see God's work and know He doesn't make mistakes!

I put my focus on my heavenly Father, seeing I do all I can to get to know Him
And when our time is come, others will see why I stayed single, and why the Father kept me, and they will no longer condemn.

Going about, 'HIS', ways and His will daily; I must be about my Father's business.
Though I'm going through training, I'm positioning myself so my purpose in life, Him and you, I won't miss!

That's how you're going to come about; I know you're in ministry in some way
And when we're joined together, we will become one and stay that way until that Great Day!

I will allow Him to wash, cleanse, and heal me, but it will take time
To be pure and ready for the season to birth our spiritually clean bloodline.

Knowing that at the same time you're going through this process too,
Purifying you as well, and we'll meet up when our process is through.

And my spirit will know your spirit, and know that you are the one,
For you will know too that I'm the one, because He will tell you, "My son, your search is done!"

One day you and I will meet up and come to be, both living for God,
Showing the world, this is how He said marriage is to be.

For God Himself will direct you to me,
Becoming one, living out our purpose to complete, then going home to eternity.

Printed in the United States
By Bookmasters